GENETICS

Investigating the Function of Genes
and the Science of Heredity

TREVOR DAY

rosen publishing's
**rosen
central**

New York

This edition first published in 2013 by:

The Rosen Publishing Group, Inc.
29 East 21st Street
New York, NY 10010

Copyright © 2013 by Brown Bear Books Ltd

Consultant: Don Franceschetti, Ph.D., Distinguished Service Professor, Departments of Physics and Chemistry, The University of Memphis, Memphis, Tennessee

Creative Director: Jeni Child
Picture Researcher: Helen Simm
Illustrators: Darren Awuah,
    Richard Burgess, and Mark Walker
Managing Editor: Tim Harris
Children's Publisher: Anne O'Daly
Production Director: Alastair Gourlay
Editorial Director: Lindsey Lowe

Library of Congress Cataloging-in-Publication Data

Day, Trevor.
Genetics: investigating the function of genes and the science of heredity/Trevor Day.—1st ed.
p. cm.—(Scientific pathways)
Includes bibliographical references and index.
ISBN 978-1-4488-7199-5 (library binding)
1. Genetics—Juvenile literature. 2. Heredity—Juvenile literature. I. Title.
QH437.5.D392 2012
576.5—dc23

2011047887

Manufactured in the United States of America

CPSIA Compliance Information: Batch #S12YA: For further information, contact Rosen Publishing, New York, New York, at 1-800-237-9932.

CONTENTS

<u>INTRODUCTION</u>

Genetics is the scientific study of how living things inherit their features. In people, genetics controls the characteristics that make us who we are, from height and eye color to the chances of contracting diseases.

IN PAST TIMES, SOME PEOPLE believed that only the environment outside the body helped shape the features of the unborn. Many thought that the characteristics of offspring were the result of the simple mixing of fluids from the mother and father. Also widespread was the notion that some living things could arise from dead or nonliving things, such as maggots from rotten meat or frogs from mud.

In the nineteenth century, scientists established that young inherit their features from factors carried in cells from the father (sperm) and mother (eggs). In the 1860s, Gregor Mendel, an Austrian monk who bred pea plants, discovered some basic laws of genetics: Young inherit their features as genes that come in pairs. Genes are passed on from generation to generation. In the early twentieth century, scientists

found that chromosomes—stringlike structures inside cells—carry genes. By the 1950s they knew that DNA makes up genes. In 1953, James Watson and Francis Crick figured out the structure of DNA. They and others suggested how DNA might unwind to make copies of itself, and how it carried a genetic code. Many people think the unraveling of the structure and function of DNA was the most important advance in twentieth-century biology.

By the 1970s, geneticists were using microorganisms such as bacteria to cut and paste sections of DNA. Scientists could then insert genes from one organism into another. By the 1980s, genetic engineering was big business. Drug companies inserted human genes into microorganisms to make medicines. Other companies were inserting genes into plants to make them more resistant to disease and to yield a better crop.

In 1990, geneticists across the world began to figure out the entire sequence of human genes. Such knowledge will help future scientists use gene therapy to repair or replace genes that cause diseases. Genetically modified food crops and gene therapy offer great opportunities, but they also raise many questions about how far scientists should go when tampering with nature.

1 MYTHS, LEGENDS, AND SUPERSTITIONS

In ancient times, physicians, philosophers, and farmers all had their own ideas about how parents passed on characteristics to their young. In the nineteenth century, scientists figured out that cells carried the inherited factors.

SINCE ANCIENT TIMES, PEOPLE have wondered how they inherited their features. Myths, legends, superstitions, and religions all included ideas about inheritance. By around 8000 BCE, farmers in the Middle East and Asia had begun to farm wheat, barley, and rice, and breed goats, sheep, and cattle.

LABAN'S FLOCK OF GOATS

Many early thinkers believed that magical forces in the environment shaped the features of offspring while they were still inside the mother. In the Bible, Genesis Chapter 30 describes how Laban's flock of dark goats gave rise to black-and-white speckled young (below). The Bible says this is because Jacob set out white willow rods near Laban's flock. According to the story, the rods magically affected the color of the goat kids. A modern scientific explanation would be that dark goats contain hidden genetic factors for light coloration. Such hidden factors often become expressed (visible) in later generations.

SPONTANEOUS GENERATION

People used to believe that maggots sprang miraculously from rotten meat, and frogs and toads (above) grew out of mud. If this were the case, these animals could not have inherited their features from their parents. In 1864, French chemist Louis Pasteur (1822–1895) showed that nonliving matter sterilized by heat and then kept sealed from the atmosphere never gave rise to living things. Pasteur had proved that spontaneous generation did not occur.

THE LAWS OF MANU

Early Hindus noted that some diseases, such as asthma or heart disease, can run in the family. They took this idea a stage further and believed that children inherited all the physical and mental characteristics of their parents. Under this idea, leaders produced children who were born to be leaders and the "lowly born" would have children who were suited to be followers. According to the laws of Manu (a Hindu god), "A man of base descent can never escape his origins." Such thinking shaped the caste system that still exists in parts of India. Under the caste system, people inherit a set place in society and do certain jobs. For example, members of a high caste may all be rulers, while people in a lower caste may all be garbage collectors. In some cases, members of different castes may not be allowed to marry.

Farmers carried out the first genetic experiments by selective breeding, or choosing individuals to breed from. They saved seeds from wheat plants that grew fastest and gave the largest crop. By sowing seeds from only the most useful plants, the farmers produced faster-growing and higher-yielding crops in the next generation. The first livestock farmers took animals from the wild. By breeding from only the wooliest and tamest sheep, farmers produced domestic sheep different in appearance and behavior from their wild ancestors. Early farmers realized that results from selective breeding of

CELLS

Using microscopes, many investigators began to find that living organisms contained tiny compartments called cells. By the early nineteenth century, biologists recognized that living organisms are built of cells. Many microorganisms (microscopic organisms), such as bacteria (right), are made up of just one cell. More complex organisms—such as fish, people, and trees—are formed by billions of cells.

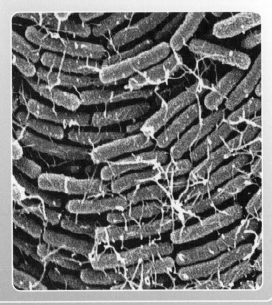

Bacteria are microscopic, single-celled organisms.

animals were difficult to predict. Even pure-breeding strains, such as dark cattle that when bred always seemed to produce dark offspring, would occasionally produce different colored calves. Crossing a white goat with a black one would not yield young that were gray. The young might be all black, all white, or a speckled mix. When farmers bred two strains together, the offspring (hybrids) were rarely an average or simple mix of the two parents. As stories in the Bible and laws in early Hindu texts show, people did not know why this happened.

Some of the great thinkers of ancient Greece turned their attention to inheritance. The philosopher Socrates (469–399 BCE) noted that many able Greek statesmen produced sons who grew up to become lazy and disruptive. Clearly, not all human qualities were inherited. The famous doctor Hippocrates (c. 460–357 BCE) guessed correctly that the father's contribution to a child's inherited features was carried in his reproductive fluid, called semen. Hippocrates then went on to suggest—incorrectly—that women produced a similar fluid. He thought that the blend of these fluids determined the child's features. The philosopher Aristotle (384–322 BCE) believed that the male's semen gave form to the baby. Aristotle mistakenly thought that babies would be boys unless the mother's blood caused interference and created a female. No one knew that living things were made from cells, or that mammals had eggs.

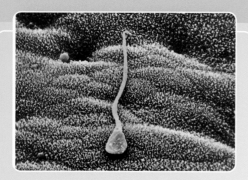

SEMEN AND SPERM

No one in ancient Greece knew that semen contained sperm cells. Centuries later, Antoni van Leeuwenhoek (1632–1723) invented the microscope and became the first person to see sperm cells (above) in detail. He believed that each sperm cell contained a miniature human being that would grow in size to become a baby. Leeuwenhoek's idea would mean that miniature males in sperm must contain even tinier sperm, which themselves contain even tinier people, and so on.

HARVEY'S EGG HUNT

Mammals are air-breathing, backboned animals that have hair and suckle their young with milk. They include cats, deer, and people. No one had ever seen mammalian eggs, but English doctor William Harvey (1578–1657) thought they must exist. He dissected several dozen of the king's deer but failed to find any eggs inside. This is not surprising, because the single-celled eggs of almost all mammals are tiny.

An illustration from Harvey's book about his search for mammal eggs.

Gulielmus Harveus
de
Generatione Animalium.

SEXUAL ANIMALS

Many animals are sexual. Sexual animals have both male and female individuals. Males release reproductive cells called sperm cells; females produce egg cells. The sperm swim to meet the egg. The first sperm to enter the egg fertilizes it (right; upper). After fertilization, the combined egg and sperm cell divides (right; lower) many times to create a new individual. In mammals, the female sex organs that produce eggs are called ovaries. Eggs from the ovaries are released into tubes called oviducts. Males produce sperm in their testes and release them in a fluid called semen. The male delivers sperm into the female through his penis.

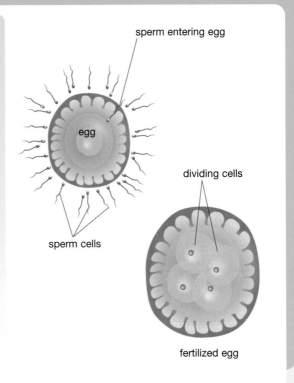

sperm entering egg

egg

sperm cells

dividing cells

fertilized egg

Until the European Middle Ages, many people in different cultures believed, correctly, that "like begat like"—cattle produced calves, pigs gave birth to piglets, people produced children. In medieval Europe, however, many people thought evil people gave birth to all kinds of animals, from bats to cats. The idea that living creatures grew out of nonliving things (spontaneous generation) was common.

Progress in the study of the fluids or factors that were passed from parents to young advanced greatly after the invention of the microscope. Dutch scientist Antoni van Leeuwenhoek (1632–1723) was the first to develop a simple but powerful microscope. Using this device, he became the first person to see individual human sperm cells in semen. To Leeuwenhoek, the sperm cells looked like tiny worms.

While Leeuwenhoek was watching sperm, William Harvey (1578–1657), physician to the king of England, was searching for mammal eggs.

Many years later, in 1827, the German scientist Karl Ernst von Baer (1792–1876) used a microscope to see a dog egg cell. In 1875, Oscar Hertwig (1849–1922) observed fertilization, when a sperm and an egg cell fuse, in animals. This also occurs in plants. Biologists then understood that two reproductive cells join to form a single cell, called a zygote. The zygote divides many times to create a new individual. If people wanted to find the factors that carried inherited characteristics, they needed to look inside cells.

LOOKING INSIDE CELLS

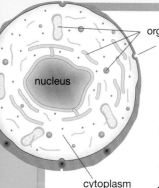

organelles
cell membrane
nucleus
cytoplasm

Most cells are tiny. The human egg cell is a very large cell, yet it is only about the size of the period at the end of this sentence. Although small, cells have a complicated structure, which becomes visible only when the cell is stained with chemical dyes. A typical animal cell (left) has an outer skin called the cell membrane, a DNA-containing control center called the nucleus, and a gel-like substance between the nucleus and the cell membrane called the cytoplasm. The cytoplasm contains many different organelles (tiny organs) that perform numerous functions, such as storing energy and making proteins.

SEXUAL PLANTS

anther
(male part)

stigma
(female part,
contains
ovaries)

Around 1700, the German botanist Rudolf Camerarius (1665–1721) showed that plant flowers have sexual organs. Male parts called anthers inside the flowers shed pollen. Each grain of dustlike pollen contains a sperm cell. Pollen travels on the wind or is carried by an insect to the female part of a flower, called the stigma. When this happens, the flower has been pollinated. Later researchers showed that a settled pollen grain grows toward an egg-containing ovary and releases a sperm cell. The sperm cell fertilizes (fuses with) a female egg cell, which develops into a seed. The seed may sprout in soil and grow into a plant.

2 | A MONK'S PEAS

Nineteenth-century biologists were a little closer to figuring out how inheritance worked than earlier investigators. Then the plant-breeding experiments of an Austrian monk laid the foundation of genetics.

IN THE LATE 1850s, THE scientific world was buzzing about Charles Darwin's ideas on evolution, which he had published in 1859 in his revolutionary book *On the Origin of Species by Means of Natural Selection*.

Biologists then believed that animals and plants inherited a simple mix of fluids from their parents. The mix gave young their characteristics. Offspring were the average of their parents. Even Charles Darwin thought so.

CHARLES DARWIN

Charles Darwin (1809–1882; left) was the developer, as well as Alfred Russel Wallace (1823–1913), of the theory of evolution by means of natural selection. According to this theory, those individuals that are best adapted to the environment are the ones most likely to breed and pass on their characteristics. Unless environmental conditions change, these characteristics are likely to spread through the population. Darwin carried out breeding experiments with garden peas and snapdragons. Like others before him, Darwin could not find a simple genetic explanation for his results.

GREGOR MENDEL

Gregor Mendel (1822–1884; right) became a monk at the age of twenty-one. He later studied natural science and mathematics at a university. By breeding pea plants, which he called his "children," Mendel discovered many of the simpler, or classical, laws of genetics. In later life, he became abbot of the monastery. The pressure of his duties meant that Mendel had to give up his scientific research.

BREEDING PLANTS AND TYPES OF POLLINATION

Many plants—including the peas bred by Mendel—produce flowers that have both male and female parts. Often, the pollen from the male parts of a flower on one plant pollinate the female parts of a flower on another plant. This process is called cross-pollination. Individual pea plants, however, also pollinate themselves. This process is called self-pollination. Plant breeders such as Gregor Mendel used paintbrushes to transfer pollen from one flower to another. In this way they could control whether a plant self-pollinated or cross-pollinated with a plant of the breeder's choice.

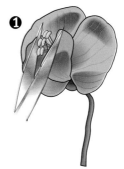

❶

1. Mendel removed the anthers from his pea flowers to ensure they did not pollinate themselves and spoil his results.

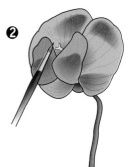

❷

2. Then Mendel used a paintbrush to transfer pollen to the pea flower from a plant of his choice.

Biologists at the time were most interested in the really big genetic question—how does a single cell, the fertilized egg, develop to become an entire adult? No one seemed to be performing experiments to find out the rules of genetics. No one, that is, except for a quiet and, at the time, almost unknown Austrian monk named Gregor Mendel.

When he performed his experiments, Mendel did several things that other biologists had not done before. First, he carried out his plant-breeding experiments with a simple organism, the pea plant. Second, he studied only one or a few features at a time, such as seed color or shape, and flower color. Third, Mendel used pure-breeding strains of plants. These plants, when self-pollinated, almost always yielded young with the same features as themselves. For example, parent plants with white flowers produced young plants with white flowers.

Mendel experimented by breeding different pure-breeding strains of peas —such as those with white flowers and those with purple ones—and carefully noted the results. Finally, he carefully counted the different types of offspring.

Mendel's work was far in advance of his time. When he published his results in 1866, he sent copies of his scientific paper to leading biologists. None realized the importance of the paper, and all ignored his work. Mendel's pioneering findings went unnoticed until the end of the nineteenth century. Then, three scientists in different countries were all working on genetics. They checked science libraries for the

ONE OF MENDEL'S EXPERIMENTS

Mendel crossed pure-breeding plants that produced smooth seeds with those that had wrinkled ones. The offspring plants did not yield peas that were the average of their parents—slightly wrinkled. Instead, all their seeds were smooth. When Mendel crossed these first-generation offspring with each other, however, they produced second-generation offspring that had peas that were either smooth or wrinkled. About three-quarters of the plants had smooth peas and one-quarter wrinkled peas. The smooth seed genetic factor (called dominant) masked the presence of the wrinkled-pea factor (called recessive). The ratio of dominant and recessive characters is always three to one in this example.

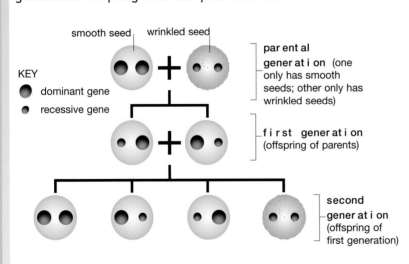

smooth seed · wrinkled seed

KEY
● dominant gene
• recessive gene

parental generation (one only has smooth seeds; other only has wrinkled seeds)

first generation (offspring of parents)

second generation (offspring of first generation)

published work of earlier scientists. All three stumbled across Mendel's 1866 paper. To their surprise, they discovered he had beaten them to an explanation of genetic inheritance by more than thirty years. Mendel showed that pea plants' characteristics were passed on by simple genetic factors, which he called particles (much later, biologists named the particles genes). A plant carries two copies of a gene.

One comes from the male parent and is carried in the pollen grain. The other comes from the female parent and is located in the egg cell. In pure-bred plants, whose ancestors are all of the same type, both copies of the gene are the same. Mendel's laws of inheritance showed that inherited features of the offspring came from each parent, but were not the result of blending characteristics from both parents.

MENDEL'S LAWS OF INHERITANCE

- Inherited features are determined by genetic factors that remain separate—factors from each parent do not blend.
- One form of a genetic factor may be dominant over another. The weaker form, called recessive, is not destroyed and may reveal itself in later generations.
- Each inherited characteristic is determined by at least two genetic factors, with one factor inherited from each parent.
- Characteristics of different kinds—such as flower or pea color—are inherited separately. For example, an individual with genetic factors for white flowers could just as easily carry the genetic factor for green seeds as for yellow seeds.

Later scientists proved that Mendel had too simple a view of his last rule. Genes for some characteristics are linked and can be inherited together.

3 FROM FRUIT FLIES TO PEOPLE

Between the early 1900s and the 1930s, geneticists made great advances in discovering how genes are inherited. Many of their experiments involved the tiny fruit fly.

IN 1879, GERMAN BIOLOGIST Walther Flemming (1843–1905) stained cells and discovered dark grains in the nucleus of the cells. He called the grains chromatin, from the Greek word for "color." By 1882, he found that chromatin turned into strands that split and moved apart when a

CHROMOSOMES

Every organism has thousands of different genetic factors (genes) that give it all its characteristics. Each organism has only a certain number of chromosomes in its cells. For example, human cells have twenty-three pairs (below) and pea plant cells have seven pairs, while fruit fly cells have only four. Biologists soon realized that each chromosome must carry many genes.

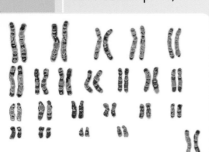

THOMAS HUNT MORGAN

Wildlife and fossils fascinated Thomas Hunt Morgan (1866–1945; below) as a child. In his adult life as a biologist, Morgan assembled a team of scientific researchers to study genetics in the fruit fly. The team remained at the forefront of genetic research for more than twenty years. In 1933, Morgan (right) was awarded a Nobel Prize for his contribution to the science of genetics.

WHY STUDY THE FRUIT FLY?

There are many reasons why Thomas Hunt Morgan chose to study fruit fly genetics. First, fruit flies have only four pairs of chromosomes in their cells. Second, fruit flies have huge chromosomes in cells in their salivary glands. (These glands are organs that make saliva.) The chromosomes are easy to observe under a microscope. Fruit flies also breed quickly, are easy to keep, and take up little space in the laboratory. Lastly, fruit flies have dozens of inherited characteristics that are easy to observe and study.

Part of a fruit fly chromosome magnified.

These bands are associated with genes for eye color.

This band is associated with genes for bristle development.

MALE AND FEMALE

Morgan and his colleagues found that the female fruit fly had four matched pairs of chromosomes. Males, however, had three matched pairs and one unmatched pair. The unmatched chromosomes are called X and Y. Females carry two X chromosomes but have no Y chromosome. XX individuals are female. They produce egg cells that carry an X chromosome. XY individuals are male. They produce sperm cells that carry either an X or a Y chromosome. Whether or not the male's sperm contains an X or Y chromosome determines the offspring's gender. A similar way of determining gender from inheriting the father's X or Y chromosome occurs in many other animals, including humans.

cell divided. Later researchers called these strands chromosomes.

In 1902, soon after the rediscovery of Mendel's laws of inheritance, American biologist Walter Sutton (1877–1916) pointed out that chromosomes, like Mendel's genetic factors, come in pairs. In both cases, one of the pair is inherited from the father and one from the mother. Sutton guessed correctly that the genetic factors that passed from parents to offspring were carried on the chromosomes. Not long after, in 1909, American biologist Thomas Hunt Morgan began to use the fruit fly for genetic research in his work at Columbia University, New York.

LINKED GENES

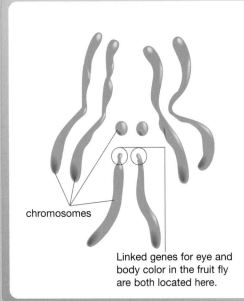

chromosomes

Linked genes for eye and body color in the fruit fly are both located here.

If genes for two different characteristics—such as eye color and body color in the fruit fly (left)—lie on the same chromosome, they are linked. Linked genes may be passed on together, unlike the flower and seed colors in pea plants that Mendel used in his famous experiments. Twentieth-century geneticists found that the closer two genes are on a chromosome, the more closely they are linked, and the more likely they are to be inherited together. Linked genes provide geneticists with a way to map the position of genes on chromosomes.

Morgan and his colleagues made many important discoveries, including how an animal's gender is inherited and how genes are linked.

In 1905, British biologist William Bateson (1861–1926) called the study of inheritance genetics, from the Greek word meaning "to generate." In 1909, Danish plant biologist Wilhelm Johannsen (1857–1927) gave Mendel's genetic factors the name genes. By the 1910s, it was clear that many genetic traits in fruit flies, and some in other animals

such as cattle and mice, were inherited in the same simple way first revealed by Mendel's work with peas. There were some exceptions. Morgan and his colleagues, including Alfred Sturtevant (1891–1970), showed that genes for different characteristics can be inherited together because they are linked on the same chromosome.

In 1915, Morgan, Sturtevant, and their colleagues published the first chromosome maps. The chromosome maps showed the position of fifty genes for different characteristics scattered among the fruit fly's four pairs of chromosomes.

Breeding experiments like those that used peas and flies cannot be carried out with humans. To study genetics in people, scientists observe family trees to see how people inherit traits such as hemophilia. Such studies are particularly revealing where a group of closely related people intermarry over several generations, as happened with the related people who form the royal families of Europe.

HEMOPHILIA: A GENETIC DISEASE

Hemophilia is an inherited disease in which the blood does not clot easily. A small cut or bruise can lead to severe bleeding for a hemophiliac. The gene for hemophilia is recessive and is carried on the X chromosome. Males have only one X chromosome, so always suffer from the disease if they inherit the gene. If a female carries one copy of the hemophilia gene, it is usually masked by a normal gene on the other X chromosome. Females

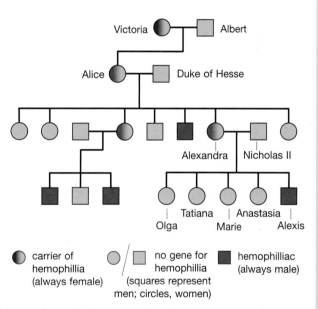

rarely suffer from hemophilia but can be carriers of the gene. Carriers can pass the condition to their children but do not have it themselves. Queen Victoria of England (1819–1901) was a carrier of the hemophilia gene. She passed on the gene to two of her daughters. One daughter, named Alice, married and had a daughter, named Alexandra, who also carried the gene. Alexandra married Czar Nicholas II of Russia. They had a son, Alexis, who suffered from the disease hemophilia.

4 THE DISCOVERY OF DNA

The discovery of the structure of DNA—the substance that makes up genes—was the most important biological advance of the twentieth century.

IN 1869, GERMAN CHEMIST Friedrich Miescher (1844–1895) described a substance he found in a cell nucleus. He visited hospital wards and collected patients' bandages stained with pus (the yellowish liquid that oozes from infected wounds) to obtain large amounts of the substance. The pus contained large numbers of white blood cells from which Miescher took the substance. He called it nuclein. It was later renamed nucleic acid.

OSWALD AVERY

Canadian-born scientist Oswald Avery (1877–1955; left) lived in New York for most of his life. He trained as a medical doctor before he turned to medical research. Avery was dedicated to both his work and his colleagues but shunned publicity. Avery lived only yards away from his workplace at Rockefeller Institute Hospital and rarely left New York.

NUCLEIC ACIDS

There are two main kinds of nucleic acids in a cell: DNA and RNA. DNA is found mostly in the nucleus of cells. RNA is found both in the nucleus and in other parts of the cell.

A model of the structure of DNA.

In the 1920s, biological chemists were looking for chemicals that might make up the genes in chromosomes. They found that chromosomes contain nucleic acid and protein. Biologists thought that protein was the most likely genetic material. Proteins contain twenty kinds of building blocks, called amino acids. Nucleic acids contain just four kinds of building blocks, called nucleotides.

In 1944, Oswald Avery (1877–1955) and his colleagues proved a nucleic acid called DNA was the genetic material. His team grew colonies of pneumonia bacteria. Some colonies were harmless to mice but others were deadly. Avery and his team took DNA from the deadly bacteria and introduced it to the harmless ones. The harmless bacteria became deadly, showing that the DNA carried the code for deadliness.

CHROMOSOMES

X-shaped chromosome

DNA coils up

DNA

Chromosomes, including those of people, are made up of strands of the nucleic acid DNA (*see* page 22). In an animal cell, DNA replicates (copies itself) and then winds around itself again and again to form an X-shaped chromosome (above). People have forty-six chromosomes. They get twenty-three from their mom, and twenty-three from their dad. (Only four are shown in this simplified artwork, right, for convenience.) Male and female sex cells (sperm and eggs) contain only twenty-three chromosomes each, half the normal amount. When a sperm and an egg fuse, they produce a fertilized cell that develops into a new person who has forty-six chromosomes.

dad (46)

mom (46)

sperm and eggs (23)

offspring (46)

BACTERIA

Bacteria are single-celled microorganisms. Most are about one-hundredth the width of the period at the end of this sentence. They have a simple cell structure with no nucleus. Their DNA makes a single circular chromosome. Their simple structure and rapid rate of reproduction make bacteria useful in genetics experiments.

DNA has to do at least two things to be the genetic material. First, it must be able to make exact copies of itself. This enables the DNA to pass intact to new cells when a cell divides. Second, DNA must carry a code that gives the organism its characteristics. By the early 1950s, teams of scientists in Europe and America were trying to determine the structure of DNA.

James Watson teamed up with Francis Crick in Cambridge, England. At King's College, London, the chemist Rosalind Franklin was working with

FROM CRICK AND WATSON TO DNA REPLICATION

Francis Crick (1916–2004) began his scientific career as a physicist before he began to study the structure of proteins and DNA. He also predicted the nature of the genetic, or triplet, code and how RNA might be involved in making proteins (see page 24). Others later proved many of Crick's ideas. Chicago-born James Watson (born 1928) entered college when he was only fifteen years old. In 1951, he began to study at the University of Cambridge, England, and soon teamed up with Francis Crick. Together they discovered the structure of DNA, for which Crick, Watson, and Maurice Wilkins received the Nobel Prize in 1962. After Crick and Watson presented the structure of DNA, others used their work to figure out how DNA replicates (copies itself).

A molecule of DNA is made up of two long strands. The strands are connected by four different bases (A, C, G, and T). Each of the four bases fits with only one other, its partner. A always pairs with T, and G always pairs with C. If a base pair separates, only another partner base can fill the gap. The two strands of DNA can unzip by separating their base pairs. Each unzipped strand re-creates its missing half and forms a new DNA molecule: Unattached partner bases link to each base on the unzipped strands and form two new strands of DNA. The DNA in a cell doubles in this way before the cell divides in two. One copy of the DNA ends up in each new cell. This ensures that every body cell carries the same DNA.

DNA double helix

"unzipped" DNA strand

bases

Bases:
- A (adenine)
- C (cytosine)
- G (guanine)
- T (thymine)

replicated DNA

X-RAY CRYSTALLOGRAPHY

Rosalind Franklin fired X-rays at a crystal of DNA using a machine like the one in this picture. The X rays bounced off the atoms in the DNA and onto a photographic plate. The photographic pattern the X-rays made on the plate gave clues as to the position of the different parts of the DNA molecule.

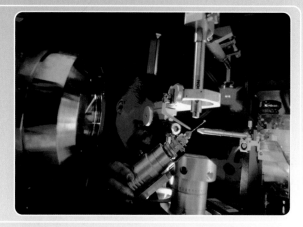

ROSALIND FRANKLIN

Rosalind Franklin (1920–1958) trained as a chemist and made advances in figuring out the structure of many carbon-based substances. Using X-ray crystallography, she revealed the spiral (helical) shape of DNA and the position of major parts. This helped Watson and Crick construct their models. Franklin later made discoveries about the structure and behavior of viruses. She died of cancer at the age of thirty-seven, before she received full credit for her contributions to genetics.

Maurice Wilkins (1916–2004) to produce photographs of DNA using a technique called X-ray crystallography. Watson and Crick made models of possible DNA structures. In 1953, after seeing Franklin's X-ray crystallography data, they built a model of DNA that changed genetics forever. Watson and Crick figured out a shape for the molecule that would best fit everything they knew about DNA. It was a double helix, which looks like a spiral staircase or a twisted ladder. The rungs of the ladder are formed by pairs of molecules called bases. There are four types of bases on DNA: adenine (A), cytosine (C), guanine (G), and thymine (T). Each type of base can bond with only one other, called its partner (*see* left).

BUILDING PROTEINS

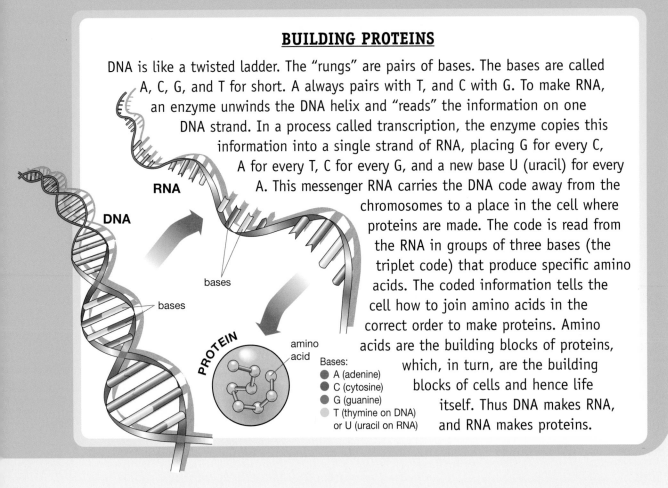

DNA is like a twisted ladder. The "rungs" are pairs of bases. The bases are called A, C, G, and T for short. A always pairs with T, and C with G. To make RNA, an enzyme unwinds the DNA helix and "reads" the information on one DNA strand. In a process called transcription, the enzyme copies this information into a single strand of RNA, placing G for every C, A for every T, C for every G, and a new base U (uracil) for every A. This messenger RNA carries the DNA code away from the chromosomes to a place in the cell where proteins are made. The code is read from the RNA in groups of three bases (the triplet code) that produce specific amino acids. The coded information tells the cell how to join amino acids in the correct order to make proteins. Amino acids are the building blocks of proteins, which, in turn, are the building blocks of cells and hence life itself. Thus DNA makes RNA, and RNA makes proteins.

RNA

DNA

bases

bases

PROTEIN

amino acid

Bases:
- A (adenine)
- C (cytosine)
- G (guanine)
- T (thymine on DNA) or U (uracil on RNA)

For DNA to be able to carry instructions, scientists thought it must form a code like a string of letters. The code was laid out along the length of a DNA strand. Watson, Crick, and others realized that the code was carried by the repeated combinations of the bases. To give enough combinations, the code on the double helix must be batches of three letters, such as AAT, AGC, and TAC. Three letters can be combined in sixty-four different ways. This gives more than enough combinations to code for all twenty different amino acids, the building blocks of proteins.

In the mid-1960s, several scientists working with bacteria, including American Marshall Nirenberg (born 1927) and Indian American Gobind Khorana (born 1922), found that several groups of three letters give the code for the same amino acid. For example, CCA, CCG, CCT, and CCC all code for one amino acid. They also found that three of the letter groups act as periods to mark the end of a gene.

In the early 1960s, molecular geneticists figured out the role of the other nucleic acid, RNA. In plant and animal cells, RNA carries the genetic message from the DNA in the nucleus to places in the cell where proteins are made. In effect, RNA is the messenger that delivers plans for building proteins from the DNA controller.

In 1941, George Beadle (1903–1989) and Edward Tatum (1909–1975) suggested that each gene produces its characteristics by constructing a type of protein called an enzyme.

ENZYMES

Enzymes are biological catalysts, which speed or trigger chemical reactions in the body but remain unchanged. There are many different enzymes in an organism, all doing their own specific tasks. For example, the color of a person's eyes (right) is determined by enzymes involved in making eye pigments. By the 1950s, experiments by other researchers lent plenty of support to Beadle's and Tatum's theory that one gene produces one enzyme. Today, scientists know that sometimes more than one gene is needed to produce one enzyme.

5 MAPPING DNA

Between the 1950s and 1980s, geneticists began to apply what they had learned about microorganisms to tackle the challenge of mapping the DNA in plants and animals.

BY THE 1950S, BIOLOGISTS WERE routinely studying bacteria and viruses in the laboratory and carrying out genetic experiments with them. Some began to map the genes on the DNA of the bacterium *Escherichia* *coli* (*E. coli*, a bacterium that lives in the human intestine). Their results were confusing until, in 1954, American researcher Ruth Sager (1918–1997) suggested correctly that the bacterium might have circular

BACTERIA AND PLASMIDS

Bacteria (singular bacterium) are tiny organisms made up of a single cell each (*see* pages 8 and 21). The cell is surrounded by an elastic cell membrane and a tougher outer cell wall. Some bacteria have whiplike flagella (singular flagellum) that they spin to propel themselves. Inside the cell, a bacterium's genetic material is a long strand of

flagellum

cell membrane

cell wall | DNA | plasmid

cytoplasm

DNA that is joined at both ends. It forms a dense mass but is not contained within a membrane-enclosed nucleus as in animal cells (*see* page 11). This bacterial DNA is also called a chromosome, although it is different from an animal's chromosome because it is circular and is not present inside a nuclear compartment. Plasmids are small rings of DNA that are located in the cell's cytoplasm, separate from a bacterium's main DNA. Bacterial plasmids can take up cut pieces of animal or plant DNA and copy them as though they were the plasmids' own DNA. Geneticists use plasmids to copy and transfer sections of DNA (*see* page 28).

VIRUSES

A virus is even smaller and simpler than a bacterium. Viruses are tiny infectious particles that are not even cells. Many biologists do not consider viruses living things. Each virus comprises a strand of RNA or DNA wrapped in a coat of protein. Viruses called bacteriophages invade bacteria. Bacteriophages are particularly useful to geneticists since they can be used to inject DNA into a bacterium. The way a virus's RNA or DNA affects the DNA of other organisms helps scientists learn about the structure and function of DNA.

A bacteriophage virus.

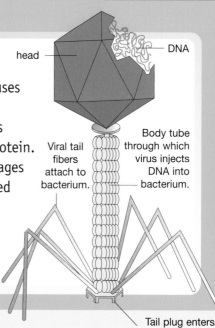

head — DNA

Viral tail fibers attach to bacterium.

Body tube through which virus injects DNA into bacterium.

Tail plug enters bacterium.

strands of DNA, not long ones like those in the nucleus of animal and plant cells.

By the early 1960s, molecular biologists were working more and more with the molecules of DNA, RNA, and proteins. One challenge was to read the sequence of bases in DNA to produce a map of genes. This work updated that of Morgan and others, who fifty years earlier had mapped genes on chromosomes. Now, however, scientists had molecular tools.

The molecules of DNA in most animals and plants are huge compared to those of microorganisms. For example, *E. coli* has about four thousand genes. The width of its DNA is only just visible with the most powerful microscopes, but its total

RNA

RNA and DNA are both nucleic acids. In some viruses, RNA is the hereditary material; however, not only viruses but also other organisms, including plants and people, have RNA in their cells. In these organisms RNA acts as a messenger, carrying a code from the DNA to areas of the cell that make proteins (*see* page 24). RNA contains three of the same bases as DNA (A, T, and C), but instead of T, RNA has a base called U (uracil).

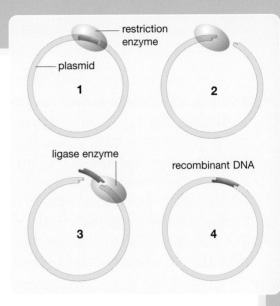

RECOMBINANT DNA

When a bacterium becomes infected by a virus, the virus inserts its own DNA into the circle of the bacterium's DNA. The bacterium defends itself by cutting out the viral DNA using molecular "scissors" called restriction enzymes. Scientists found they could use restriction enzymes to cut up DNA into short lengths. Later researchers discovered bacterial enzymes called ligases that could join the pieces of DNA. Researchers could now cut and paste sections of DNA. The first geneticists to make recombinant DNA, or DNA combined from two different sources, were Herbert Boyer (born 1936) and Stanley Cohen (born 1935). In 1973, they cut open a bacterial plasmid with a restriction enzyme. They then created a piece of DNA cut from another plasmid using the same type of enzyme. When they put the two pieces of DNA together, and added DNA ligase, the two pieces joined smoothly.

1. A restriction enzyme recognizes a section of DNA in a bacterium's plasmid and attaches to it.
2. The restriction enzyme cuts out the DNA.
3. A ligase enzyme inserts a new section of DNA.
4. The bacterium's DNA ring joins up again around the new section of DNA.

length is about 0.05 inch (0.1 mm). People, by contrast, have at least thirty thousand genes. Human DNA is around 6 feet (2 m) long. Its sequence contains 3,000 million bases.

By 1972, researchers had begun to cut and paste DNA using restriction enzymes and ligases. It was only a matter of time before someone took the DNA from one organism and spliced it into another to produce recombinant DNA, the method now used in most genetic engineering.

To figure out the sequence of the bases in DNA, molecular biologists need to work with many copies of exactly the same length of DNA. The production of such copies is called gene cloning. One way to do this is to insert the DNA in a plasmid to prompt a bacterium to make many copies. In the mid-1980s, Kary Mullis (born 1944) developed the polymerase chain reaction (PCR) method of copying DNA. Scientists later used PCR for sequencing DNA.

When molecular biologists began to sequence DNA from animals and plants, they got some big surprises. DNA did not match the genes that gave organisms their characteristics in a simple way. It became clear that genes were not single units on a chromosome. Genes were often scattered around the length of a DNA molecule. The scientists were also surprised to find that a lot of the DNA seemed to serve no purpose at all. Molecular biologists called the unused sections junk DNA.

PCR

The PCR (polymerase chain reaction) enables tiny amounts of DNA to be analyzed. Trace amounts of DNA almost too small to detect might be found at the scene of a crime, for example. PCR can make trillions of copies of just a single DNA molecule. It relies on the ability of DNA to copy itself using the enzyme DNA polymerase. Scientists heat the DNA molecule until the base pairs separate. This creates two separate strands of DNA. Then, the scientists add DNA polymerase and DNA building blocks to the mix. Each strand of DNA then recreates its missing half. The process is repeated until enough DNA has been produced.

SEQUENCING DNA

To sequence DNA is to figure out the order of its bases (A, G, C, and T). There are different ways to do this. In one, scientists generate many copies of a single strand of DNA using PCR. They add a marker particle to one end of each strand. The strands are then divided into four batches. A restriction enzyme that cuts DNA at either an A, G, C, or T base is added to each batch. This creates fragments of different lengths. The scientists then sort the fragments by length. The scientists know which base is at the end of a length since they know at which base the length was cut. The marker particle tells them how far from the start of the sequence that end base is. Using this information, scientists can figure out the sequence of bases on the original DNA sample.

These fragments of cut DNA have been sorted by length. This reveals that part of the original DNA's base sequence is A, A, C, G.

29

6 GENETIC ENGINEERING

Pharmaceutical companies use genetically engineered bacteria to produce drugs, farmers harvest genetically engineered food crops, and now medical researchers are learning how to repair or replace genes that cause disease.

GENETIC ENGINEERING IS THE use of molecular techniques to alter the genetic material of organisms, creating individuals that would never occur naturally. By the early 1980s, pharmaceutical companies were eager to use genetic engineering to make medically useful drugs inexpensively and in large amounts. Researchers spliced human genes into bacteria and

GENETICALLY ENGINEERED DRUGS

Insulin is a hormone that controls the amount of sugar in the blood. People who suffer from a disease called diabetes lack insulin and poorly control their blood sugar levels. Diabetics (people suffering from diabetes) inject insulin (right) to control their condition. Without it they might die. Drug companies previously gathered insulin from dead pigs. Genetic engineers used the bacterium *E. coli* to make human insulin, which is now available more cheaply and in greater quantities than before.

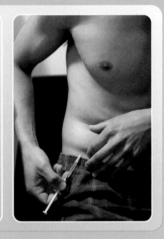

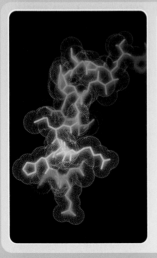

HUMAN GROWTH HORMONE

Human growth hormone (HGH) controls people's growth. Some people do not produce enough HGH for them to grow to their full potential size. Researchers genetically engineered sheep to contain the human gene that produces HGH. The engineered sheep produce HGH in their milk, which is harvested for the hormone. Before this development, HGH was expensive and in short supply, but now it is much more readily available.

A model of the chemical structure of human growth hormone.

GENETIC MONSTERS?

Some people fear that genetic engineering is creating dangerous strains of bacteria that could escape from the laboratory and endanger people or harm the environment. From the beginning, scientists have developed weakened strains of microorganisms to prevent this from happening. For example, laboratory strains of *E. coli* are now so weak that they cannot survive in the human intestine from which their ancestors originally came. Other people have moral or religious objections to genetic engineering. They view animals such as the featherless chicken (right) as unnatural monsters.

turned them into living factories to make human proteins such as HGH.

Some people fear that genetic engineering might create genetic monsters or harmful microorganisms. Scientists and governments since the 1970s have tried to control what kinds of research genetic engineers undertake, to try to curb the most dangerous uses of genetic engineering. Genetic engineering has great potential to improve the world's food supply by engineering crops with improved yields. The most common method introduces new genes into a plant using an infectious bacterium that has been made harmless. Instead of causing infectious disease, the bacterium infects the crops with new genes useful to farmers.

In the 1980s, American researchers inserted genes from a soil bacterium

ENVIRONMENTAL DANGERS

Some scientists and many environmentalists are concerned greatly about genetically engineered crops (left). The crops have genes that help them grow, such as genes that protect them from herbicides or insect pests. Some people are concerned that the genes might transfer to weeds. This transfer could produce superweeds that overrun fields and which would be difficult to destroy.

into potatoes and other plants. The bacterium produces a poison that kills beetles, caterpillars, and many other insect pests. The engineered plants make the poison in their leaves, which kills the insect pests that feed on them.

Many foods eaten today contain ingredients from engineered or genetically modified (GM) plants and animals. Some people became concerned about unintended effects of

GM foods on the environment and potential risks to human health.

Agricultural companies have developed many GM food plants. Some GM plants are resistant to chemicals that kill weeds (herbicides), enabling farmers to spray herbicides to kill weeds without damaging the crops. GM potatoes will soon contain antifreeze genes from cold-water fish that make the plants more resistant to

GENE THERAPY

In 1990, American researchers carried out the first partially successful human gene therapy trials. One trial involved a young girl who suffers from severe combined immunodeficiency disease (SCID). Researchers removed some of her white blood cells, added replacement genes that could help treat her condition, and returned the modified white blood cells to her body. People with SCID have very little protection against infection and fall victim to common diseases unless they live in a germ-free bubble environment. The gene therapy greatly improved the girl's condition. Other successful trials have been carried out since.

frost damage. Future plant breeders hope to develop strains of crops that can survive in deserts or in salty soils.

Gene therapy uses genetic engineering techniques to repair or replace a damaged gene in humans to treat or cure genetic diseases. Gene therapy trials aiming to treat many conditions have, so far, had mixed results. There are several reasons why gene therapy is difficult.

A gene for a characteristic is often scattered around a DNA molecule. That makes it difficult to engineer a replacement. Human genes also tend to be large, so it is difficult to get them to the target cells where they are to work. Once there, the gene needs to be switched on. Despite the challenges, gene therapy has the potential to cure or treat millions of people.

GENETIC DISEASES

There are at least four thousand known human genetic diseases. Most are rare. Some diseases are caused by an alteration, or mutation, in a single gene. They include cystic fibrosis (a condition that causes breathing and digestive problems) and hemophilia. Some inherited mutations make people more likely to suffer from certain types of cancer. Not all mutations are so harmful. This hedgehog (right) has no color because of a natural mutation but is otherwise healthy.

7 FUTURE PROSPECTS

Scientists have now sequenced the entire set of human DNA. Nevertheless, it will be many decades before researchers understand fully how many of the genes work together to produce human characteristics.

IN 1990, JAMES WATSON PUBLICLY launched the Human Genome Project (HGP). The HGP planned to sequence the human genome by the year 2005. A rough draft was published in 2000, and a much better version in 2003, two years ahead of schedule. More than twenty countries, including governments and private companies, were involved in this staggering task.

The HGP has created an explosion in the field of genetics. Scientists now

HUMAN GENOME FACTS

- Before the HGP, scientists predicted that the human genome contained at least one hundred thousand genes. Now they know it contains fewer than forty thousand.

- More than 99 percent of DNA is the same in all people. Less than 0.3 percent is different. This seemingly tiny difference gives each of us all our individual characteristics.

- Genes make up only about 2 percent of the human genome. The rest, 98 percent, is junk DNA. Junk DNA may play important roles, but scientists do not know what those roles might be.

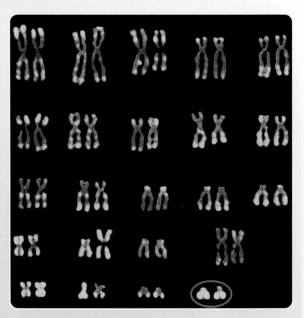

Every human cell (except eggs and sperm) carries twenty-three pairs of chromosomes. This person is a woman: The sex chromosomes (circled) are XX.

GENOME

Genome is the name for the entire set of chromosomes an individual contains and the genes that are carried on them. The human genome is made up of forty-six chromosomes, in twenty-three pairs. One of the pairs is made up of the sex chromosomes: XX in women and XY in men.

CREATING SUPERHUMANS?

Francis Galton (1822–1911; right), a cousin of Charles Darwin, believed that people of high social class should not breed with people from other classes and ethnic backgrounds. He thought that doing so would weaken the strength and purity of the race. In the 1930s and 1940s, Adolf Hitler (1889–1945) used similar arguments in seeking to breed an "Aryan super-race" of tall, blond, athletic, blue-eyed people. Eugenics has little if any support from the science of genetics. In fact, breeding between individuals of different genetic backgrounds often leads to so-called "hybrid vigor" (beneficial mixing of genes). Inbreeding, on the other hand, stifles genetic variation and so is more likely to result in offspring with inherited diseases and other abnormalities.

know the location of dozens of genes that are directly involved in disease, including cancers. The findings will help researchers look for treatments and cures, such as gene therapy. The knowledge from the HGP also opens the door to testing people for genes that cause genetic disease. Yet such advances create new challenges. How will people react if they discover they will probably suffer from a genetic disease later in life? Will it affect the jobs they are hired for, or whether medical insurance will pay for treatment? A few people fear that the new genetic knowledge will lead to selective breeding and attempts to create superhumans.

Eugenics is the theory that the human race could be improved by

CREATING DOLLY THE CLONED SHEEP

To create Dolly the sheep, researchers took unfertilized egg cells from the ovaries of a mature ewe. The scientists removed the chromosomes (DNA) from the eggs (**1**) and replaced them with chromosomes from the udder cells of another mature ewe (**2** and **3**). Then they applied electricity to the cells to fuse each nucleus into its new cell (**4**). The researchers grew the new cells in the laboratory until one formed an embryo (**5**), which they implanted in a ewe. The embryo grew to produce Dolly (**6**). It took the team 277 attempts before they had this first success. Other researchers have since cloned mice, cattle, and other animals. Despite their success with Dolly, scientists have found that cloned animals are not as healthy as animals that are bred naturally. Dolly herself died young of an age-related disease.

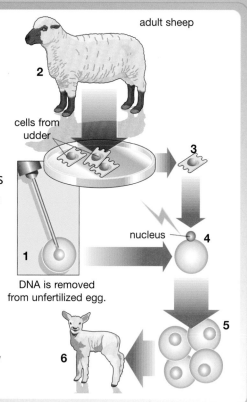

adult sheep

cells from udder

nucleus

DNA is removed from unfertilized egg.

selective breeding. People, perhaps politicians or scientists, would decide who may breed, and with whom. The theory has a long history. When human selective breeding has been attempted, the results have not been predictable.

In 1996, genetics entered a new era when a team at the Roslin Institute in Edinburgh, Scotland, created Dolly the sheep. The news was announced in 1997, when the scientists were sure

Dolly had developed normally. She was a clone (an exact genetic duplicate) grown from genetic material taken from an udder cell in an adult sheep. If a similar technique was applied to clone humans, a person could have a clone made of himself or herself.

It is most likely, however, that cloned cells will be grown outside the body to replace diseased—or repair damaged—tissues, not to create an entire human being. Cloned cells have the advantage that they are not recognized as foreign and rejected by the body for which they are designed.

New genetic techniques, such as screening for diseases, gene cloning, and animal cloning, bring not only benefits but also dilemmas. Many people are worried that old ideas of eugenics and selective breeding are returning.

Recent genetic research shows that, for example, there are no simple genes for intelligence or antisocial behavior. Human characteristics come from genes that interact in complex ways that scientists do not yet understand. A person's upbringing also plays a major role in development. Knowing the human genome is part of a long journey to discover how people develop in life.

REPAIRING DAMAGED TISSUES

Cells in the human body have many different forms and functions. Nerve cells are very different from those in muscles, the liver, or a kidney. Many nerve cells cannot divide. Liver and kidney cells do not often divide but can do so to repair damaged tissue. Stem cells are different. They are unspecialized cells that grow into new cells of many different types, enabling the body to grow and repair itself. Embryos have lots of stem cells. Genetic engineers can take the stem cells from very early stage human embryo cells and replace their chromosomes with those of a person needing treatment. The scientists could then grow the combined cell to produce, for example, replacement heart tissue. Stem cell research and therapy are controversial issues because they use human embryo cells.

WHY CLONE HUMANS?

Most people are opposed to the idea of cloning a whole person. Some of those in favor argue that it is one way of a person having a child when they cannot have one by other means. There are great difficulties involved, including an enormous waste of human embryos, to which many people object morally. Producing a cloned human is, therefore, unlikely in the immediate future. Several groups, however, acting without approval from governments or most scientists, claim to have either achieved a human clone already or to be close to success.

37

EXTRACTING DNA

GOALS
1. Separate DNA from fruit cells.
2. Observe and extract DNA from a mixture.

1 Place the bottle of denatured alcohol in the ice. The spirits must be very cold.

2 Peel the kiwi fruit, and cut it into small pieces on the chopping board. Put the pieces in the measuring cup.

WHAT YOU WILL NEED

- large bowl of ice
- bottle of denatured alcohol
- kiwi fruit
- knife and chopping board
- 2 measuring cups
- kitchen scales
- table salt
- measuring cylinder
- dishwashing liquid (not concentrated)
- water
- large saucepan of hot water
- strainer
- large spoon
- champagne flute or other tall, thin glass
- a piece of bare wire

3 Stir together ¹⁄₁₀ ounce (3g) of salt, ⅓ fluid ounce (10ml) of dishwashing liquid, and 3 fluid ounces (100ml) of water.

4 Add the dishwashing liquid–salt solution to the chopped-up fruit in the measuring cup, and let it sit for 15 minutes.

5 Put the measuring cup in the saucepan with hot water, and leave it for 15 minutes.

6 After 15 minutes hold the strainer over the glass, and pour the green mush through the strainer, catching the liquid in the glass. You will need to fill about one-fifth of the glass.

! **SAFETY TIP** *Denatured alcohol can be very dangerous if it is drunk. Ask an adult to help you during this activity.*

TROUBLESHOOTING

I did not get any DNA. What went wrong?

One possible reason is that you tried to go through the steps too quickly. Make sure to stir in the detergent for at least 15 minutes. If you let the kiwi and detergent mixture and denatured alcohol sit for 30 to 60 minutes, the DNA should precipitate (separate out) between the layers. You could also try substituting ethyl alcohol or rubbing alcohol for the denatured alcohol.

7 Very carefully drizzle the ice-cold denatured alcohol on the back of the spoon so it forms a purple layer on top of the green layer. Stop when the glass is about two-fifths full. Set the glass on the table, and watch.

8 You should see a white layer form between the green and purple liquids. It is DNA. Fish the DNA out by winding it carefully on the wire.

TIMELINE

	6000 BCE	300 CE
Atoms and Molecules	**2500** BCE Tin ore is smelted in Turkey **4th century** BCE Greek philosopher Democritus believes the world is composed of tiny particles that cannot be divided	**1450** European metalworkers work out how to separate lead and silver ores
Electricity	**271** CE The compass is first used in China; it works by detecting Earth's magnetic field	**1180** The first reference to the magnetic compass in Western writing is in Alexander Neckam's *Concerning Natural Things (De Naturis Rerum)*
Evolution		
Genetics		
Geology	**500** BCE Xenophanes of Colphon (Greece) discovers that land can rise when he finds fossils of seashells on mountaintops	**1517** The Italian scientist Girolamo Fracastoro suggests that fossils are the remains of long-dead plants and animals
Gravity	**1450** BCE Egyptians devise a water clock, based on the principle of dripping water **330** BCE Aristotle believes that the Sun and planets orbit Earth	**1345** Dutch engineers use windmills to pump water out of areas that are being reclaimed from the sea
Light	**6000** BCE People in Italy make mirrors from a rock called obsidian **1361** BCE Chinese astronomers record a solar eclipse	**1021** Arab mathematician Alhazen writes about the refraction of light **1304** Theodoric of Freibourg, a German scientist, works out how rainbows form
Medicine	**2500** BCE Chinese doctors begin using a pain-killing technique called acupuncture **1550** BCE Egyptians are using about 700 drugs and medications	**365** Mechanical cranks are used to set broken bones in Greece **850** An Arab physician writes about eye disorders and treatments
Context	**c.3500** BCE The wheel is invented in Mesopotamia **2630** BCE Egyptians begin building the pyramids **776** BCE The first Olympic Games are held in Greece **117** CE Roman Empire reaches its greatest extent	**c.900** Mayan civilization in Mesoamerica collapses **1453** The Byzantine age comes to an end with the fall of Constantinople

1709 A model hot-air balloon is made in Brazil
1714 Gabriel Fahrenheit constructs a mercury thermometer

1738 Daniel Bernoulli proposes a kinetic theory of gases
c.1787 French physicist Jacques Charles draws up Charles's Law of gas volumes

---

1701 Edmond Halley draws up a map of Earth's magnetic field
1729 Stephen Gray explains electrical conductors and insulators

1742 Benjamin Franklin demonstrates the electrical nature of lightning
1800 Alessandro Volta develops the voltaic pile electric battery

1807 Humphry Davy uses electrolysis to isolate potassium and sodium
1822 André-Marie Ampere works out the laws of the movement of electricity

---

1650 Irish archbishop James Ussher mistakenly calculates that Earth was created in 4004 BCE

1809 Lamarck wrongly states that characteristics acquired during life are inherited by offspring
1831–36 Charles Darwin on HMS *Beagle*

1760s Robert Bakewell improves farmstock by selectively breeding animals

1831 Robert Brown is the first scientist to describe a cell nucleus

---

1691 Naturalist John Ray believes fossils are ancient life-forms

1793 Mammoth remains are found in Siberian permafrost

1811 Schoolgirl Mary Anning discovers the first fossil ichthyosaur
1815 Eruption of Mount Tambora in Indonesia modifies climates worldwide

---

1609 Johannes Kepler draws up laws of planetary motion
c.1665 Isaac Newton formulates his law of gravity

1665 Robert Hooke proposes that light travels in waves
1671 Isaac Newton shows that a prism splits light into a spectrum

1811 William Wollaston invents the *camera lucida*
1839 Louis Daguerre invents a kind of photograph taken on metal plates

---

1628 Physician William Harvey explains the circulation of blood
1721 Smallpox inoculation is carried out in North America

1745 The French surgeon Jacques Daviel successfully removes a cataract from a patient's eye—the first time this has happened

1805 Japanese physician Seishu Hoanoka performs surgery with general anesthesia
1811 Charles Bell pioneers study of the nervous system

1630 English Puritans colonize Massachusetts Bay
1665 Bubonic plague kills one-fifth of London's population

1787 The United States Constitution is adopted
1789 The French Revolution begins with the storming of the Bastille

1803 The Louisiana Purchase doubles the size of the United States
1833 A law is passed in Britain to abolish slavery in the British Empire

---

1600   **1730**   **1800**   **1850**

TIMELINE

Atoms and Molecules	**1892** James Dewar invents the vacuum bottle **1896** Henri Becquerel discovers radioactivity **1897** Physicist J.J. Thompson is the first person to identify electrons	**1905** Albert Einstein publishes his special theory of relativity **1910** The existence of the nucleus of an atom is proven by Ernest Rutherford
Electricity	**1877** American engineer Thomas Edison invents the phonograph **1885** American electrical engineer William Stanley makes the first transformer	**1923** John Logie Baird makes a type of television
Evolution	**1856** Male Neanderthal skeleton found; it differs in important ways from modern human skeletons **1859** Charles Darwin publishes *On the Origin of Species*, arguing his case for evolution	**1908** Marcellin Boule reconstructs a skeleton of a Neanderthal person **1938** A coelanth "living fossil" is found in the ocean off the South African coast
Genetics	**1865** Gregor Mendel, an Austrian monk, puts forward his laws of inheritance; they are published the following year	**1909** Danish botanist Wilhelm Johannsen defines a gene **1913** Chromosome mapping is pioneered by Alfred Sturtevant
Geology	**1861** The first fossil *Archaeopteryx* is found **1883** Mount Krakatoa, in Indonesia, erupts; it is one of the largest volcanic eruptions in recorded history	**1913** Earth's age is calculated at 4.6 billion years by geologist Arthur Holmes **1935** Richter scale proposed to measure earthquake intensity
Gravity	**1851** Léon Foucault builds a pendulum (Foucault's pendulum) that shows Earth's rotation **1891** John Poynting, an English physicist, works out the value of the gravitational constant	**1927** Georges Lemaitre suggests the universe originated with a "big bang"
Light	**1877** Joseph Swan, an English physicist, develops the first electric light bulb **1882** Albert Michelson calculates the speed of light to within 0.02 percent of the correct value	**1905** Albert Einstein publishes his special theory of relativity **1935** Transparency film invented by American amateur photographers
Medicine	**1885** Louis Pasteur manufactures a rabies vaccine **1898** The cause of malaria, the protozoa *Plasmodium*, is discovered by physician Ronald Ross **1903** X-rays first used to treat cancerous tumors	**1929** Hormone estrogen first isolated **1934** Radio waves used to treat cancer **1943** Kidney dialysis machine built by Willem Kolff
Context	**1861–1865** American Civil War **1876** The Sioux Army of Sitting Bull defeats U.S. forces at the Battle of Little Bighorn **1897** The Klondike Gold Rush begins	**1901** Guglielmo Marconi makes the first transatlantic radio broadcast **1914–1918** World War I **1939–1945** World War II

1850   **1900**

1952 The first hydrogen bomb is exploded on an atoll in the central Pacific
1960 First optical identification of a quasar
1967 Domestic microwave ovens are sold in U.S.

1994 American scientists discover a subatomic particle that they call the top quark
2004 A "supersolid" is discovered by American scientists—it flows through another material without friction

1961 The first silicon chips are manufactured
1962 The first national live TV broadcast, a speech by President Truman in San Francisco
1975 First commercial personal computers sold

1990 Work begins on developing the World Wide Web
2007 American scientists create flexible batteries by weaving microscopic tubes of carbon into paper

1960 Remains of human ancestor *Homo habilis* discovered in Tanzania
1983 Fossils of a 16-million-year-old ancestor of humans are found by Meave Leakey in Africa

1993 The oldest-known human ancestor, *Ardipithecus ramidus*, is discovered by Berkeley scientists
2003 Footprints of an upright-walking human, who was alive 350,000 years ago, are found in Italy

1953 The structure of DNA is discovered by Francis Crick and James Watson
1959 Down syndrome discovered to be caused by an extra chromosome

1994 The first genetically modifed tomato is sold in the U.S.
1996 A sheep named Dolly is cloned in Edinburgh
1998 Human stem cells are grown in a laboratory
2000 Human genome is roughly mapped out

1977 Frozen body of a baby mammoth found in Siberian permafrost

1996 Signs of microscopic life are found in a meteorite that originated from Mars
1997 Fossils of *Protarchaeopteryx*, a birdlike reptile, are found
2000 The fossil remains of a dinosaur's heart are found

1957 The first satellites, Sputnik 1 and Sputnik 2, are sent into orbit around Earth by the Soviet Union
1969 Astronauts Armstrong and Aldrin "bounce" on the Moon's surface, showing that gravity is less there

1992 Scientists at the University of Pisa, Italy, make the most accurate calculation of the acceleration due to gravity

1955 Indian scientist Narinder Kapany invents optical fibers for carrying light long distances
1962 Light-emitting diode (LED) invented

1998 Lasers are first used by American dentists for drilling teeth
2005 Flashes of light are discovered to create X-rays

1950 Link between smoking and lung cancer found
1958 Ultrasound scans are introduced to examine unborn babies
1967 The first successful heart transplant

1983 The human immunodeficiency virus (HIV) is discovered
1987 The first heart-lung-liver transplant is carried out by a team of British surgeons
2000 Works begins on making the first artificial heart

1955–1975 Vietnam War
1968 Martin Luther King assassinated in Memphis
1969 Neil Armstrong and Buzz Aldrin are the first people to walk on the Moon's surface

1989 Communist regimes across Europe collapse
1997 Diana, Princess of Wales, killed in a car accident in Paris
2001 Attack on the World Trade Center in New York
2008 Barack Obama elected first African–American president of U.S.

1950   **1990**   **2010**

KEY PEOPLE

Aristotle (384–322 BCE)

Aristotle was born in Stagira, Greece, the son of a physician. When he was 17 he went to study at the Academy in Athens, which was then the greatest seat of learning in the world, before founding his own school, the Lyceum. Aristotle's writings spanned all branches of human knowledge, from zoology to politics, and made a lasting impact on the thoughts and scientific discoveries of later civilizations. In *A History of Animals* and *On the Generation of Animals,* he described the characteristics of different animal species and attempted to explain their behavior.

Karl Ernst von Baer (1792–1876)

Von Baer was an Estonian-born biologist who pioneered the study of animal embryos. He started his research working with bird embryos, but later moved to mammals. In 1827 he was the first person to describe the mammalian ovum. Bayer went on to frame four laws of animal development.

Francis Crick (1916–2004)

Crick studied in London, before going to work at the Cavendish Laboratory in Cambridge, England. There he met fellow scientists James Watson, Rosalind Franklin, and Maurice Wilkins (1916–2004) and set about studying the structure of the DNA molecule. After discovering that it is arranged in two long, twisting "ladders" wound around each other, they published their findings in the scientific journal *Nature* in 1953. Along with Watson and Wilkins, Crick was awarded the Nobel Prize for physiology or medicine in 1962.

Charles Darwin (1809–1882)

Born in Shrewsbury, England, Darwin was the son and grandson of physicians. As a young man he was appointed the naturalist on HMS *Beagle*, a ship that embarked on an expedition of discovery between 1831–1836. During that time Darwin's eyes were opened to the extraordinary variety of plant and animal life, and his views on evolution began to develop. It was only in 1858, however, that he and fellow scientist Alfred Russel Wallace jointly presented a paper on evolution to the Linnean Society in London. The following year, Darwin's book *On the Origin of Species by Means of Natural Selection* was published. It provoked a huge controversy—because some people said it went against the teachings of the Bible—but laid the foundations for modern views on animal and plant evolution. Darwin spent much of his later years studying the behavior of earthworms.

Rosalind Franklin (1920–1958)

Franklin was born in London, England, graduated with a degree in chemistry and physics in 1941, and moved to Paris at the age of 27, where she worked at the Central Government Laboratory for Chemistry. There, she gained valuable experience of X-ray diffraction, a technique that later helped her reveal the shape of molecules. After returning to England, she teamed up with Maurice Wilkins to investigate the DNA molecule. Two years later, Wilkins showed Franklin's DNA photographs to Francis Crick and James Watson, who were then able to publish their discovery of the double-helix structure of the molecule. Rosalind Franklin went on to study viruses but sadly died of cancer at the age of 38—before she could be awarded a Nobel Prize.

William Harvey (1578–1657)

Harvey went to school in Canterbury and university at Oxford, England, then spent two years traveling in Europe before studying at the University of Padua, Italy. It was from there that he graduated as a Doctor of Medicine in 1602. Harvey returned to England and became head physician at St. Bartholomew's Hospital in

London. Harvey was physician to the king of England and gave lectures on human anatomy. The achievement for which he is best known is the explanation of the circulatory system, outlined in his book *On the Motion of the Heart and Blood,* which was published at the 1628.

Hippocrates (c.460–377 BCE)

Hippocrates was born on the Greek island of Kos and probably learned medicine from his father and grandfather, both of whom were physicians. Hippocrates is widely considered to be the "Father of Medicine." He and his followers were the first to describe many diseases and medical conditions. Hippocrates is credited with being the first person to believe that there were scientific, rather than superstitious, explanations for diseases. He separated medicine from religion, arguing that disease was not a punishment inflicted by the gods but the product of environmental factors, diet, and living habits.

Antoni van Leeuwenhoek (1632–1723)

Antoni van Leeuwenhoek was born in the Dutch city of Delft. He is best known for his work on the improvement of the microscope and for his contributions toward microbiology. Using handcrafted, homemade microscopes, he was the first person to observe and describe single-celled organisms, which he originally referred to as *animalcules*. He was also the first person to record microscopic observations of muscle fibers, bacteria, and blood flow in small blood vessels.

Gregor Mendel (1822–1884)

Mendel grew up in what was then Austria (now part of the Czech Republic). As a boy he lived on a farm, and this probably sparked his interest in botany and horticulture. Difficult family circumstances meant he could not remain at college and he moved to a monastery in Brno, where he could continue to study without the

financial burden on his family. While he was in the monastery, Gregor began to experiment with pea plants and made some important discoveries regarding inheritance. In 1866 he sent his findings to the renowned Swiss botanist Karl Wilhelm von Nageli, who apparently failed to understand their significance.

Louis Pasteur (1822–1895)

Pasteur was born in Dole, France, graduated as a doctor of science at the age of 25, and taught at the University of Lille. An interest in the fermentation process led him to discover that the yeast used in brewing fed on sugars and produced alcohol and carbon dioxide. He discovered why beer sometimes turned sour, and developed a process (now called pasteurization) to prevent this. He later demonstrated that infectious diseases are caused by microscopic organisms called bacteria. Pasteur proposed ways of treating disease and produced vaccines for potentially lethal cholera and anthrax.

Alfred Sturtevant (1891–1970)

Sturtevant was born in Jacksonville, Illinois. As a boy he developed an interest in the ideas of Gregor Mendel. His own genetics research at the California Institute of Technology studied fruit flies. In 1913 he was the first person to produce a genetic map of a chromosome, that of a fruit fly.

James Watson (born 1928)

Watson was born in Chicago, where he graduated in biology in 1947. His interest in bird diversity led him to study genetics. Watson became convinced that the chemical structure of genes was of crucial importance for their biological role. In 1951 he moved to Cambridge University, England, and teamed up with Francis Crick. Together they published their findings on the structure of DNA. Along with Crick and Maurice Wilkins he was awarded a Nobel Prize in 1962.

GLOSSARY

amino acid A building block of a protein.

bacterium (plural bacteria) A simple micro-organism. It is a cell but lacks a nucleus.

catalyst A substance that speeds up a chemical reaction without being changed itself.

cell A microscopic compartment, made up of cytoplasm in a cell membrane and usually containing a nucleus, which makes up part or the whole of an organism.

chromosome A threadlike structure in cells made of proteins and DNA that carries genes.

clone A molecule, gene, cell, or organism genetically identical to another one.

cytoplasm The substance of a living cell outside the nucleus.

DNA (deoxyribonucleic acid) A molecule containing the genetic instructions, called genes, that control heredity, and which parents pass on to their offspring.

dominant A gene is dominant if it masks the effect of another gene at the same place on a chromosome.

double helix Shaped like a ladder twisted around itself again and again.

enzyme A catalyst made of protein.

eugenics The theory that the human race could be improved by controlled programs of selective breeding.

fertilization When reproductive cells fuse to form a zygote.

gene The part of a chromosome that determines a particular genetic characteristic.

genetic code The code by which information carried in DNA makes specific proteins (usually enzymes).

genetic engineering Inserting DNA from one individual into another, often using recombinant DNA technology.

genetics The scientific study of DNA and how characteristics are inherited.

genome The entire set of genes for an organism.

Human Genome Project Project to map all the genes present on human DNA.

hybrid Offspring produced by crossing two visibly different strains.

ligase A bacterial enzyme that can be used to join pieces of DNA.

mutation A change in a gene or chromosome.

nucleic acid A substance made up of many units called nucleotides. There are two forms of nucleic acid—DNA and RNA.

nucleotide A building block of a nucleic acid.

nucleus The part of the cell, enclosed by a membrane, that contains chromosomes.

plasmid A small circular piece of DNA in a bacterium or in the cytoplasm of a plant or animal cell.

pollination The transfer of pollen from the male part (anther) to the female part (stigma) of flowers.

protein A chemical substance made up of a long chain of amino acids.

recessive A gene is recessive if it is masked by the effect of a dominant gene at the same place on a chromosome.

recombinant DNA DNA from different sources that is artificially joined.

reproduction The production of more members of a species by natural means.

reproductive cells The cells of an individual that are involved in reproduction.

RNA (ribonucleic acid) Type of nucleic acid that carries the genetic message from DNA into the cytoplasm where proteins are made.

sex chromosomes Chromosomes that determine the sex (gender) of an individual.

species Population of similar individuals that interbreed to produce fertile offspring.

virus A simple particle that infects organisms. It has a protein coat surrounding DNA or RNA.

FOR MORE INFORMATION

BOOKS

Duke, Shirley. *You Can't Wear These Genes*. Vero Beach, FL: Rourke, 2011.

Hand, Carol. *Introduction to Genetics*. New York, NY: Rosen, 2011.

Hartman, Eve. *The Role of Genetics*. Chicago, IL: Raintree, 2009.

Heos, Bridget. *Human Genome*. New York, NY: Rosen, 2011.

Hyde, Natalie. *Traits and Attributes*. New York, NY: Crabtree, 2010.

McLeish, Ewan. *Genetic Revolution*. Mankato, MN: Stargazer Books, 2009.

O'Neal, Claire. *Projects in Genetics*. Hockessin, DE: Mitchell Lane, 2011.

Sandvold, Lynette Brent. *Genetics*. Tarrytown, NY: Marshall Cavendish Benchmark, 2010.

Schacter, Bernice. *Genetics in the News*. New York, NY: Chelsea House, 2007.

Schafer, Susan. *Heredity*. Armonk, NY: M.E. Sharpe, 2009.

Simpson, Kathleen. *National Geographic Investigates: Genetics.* Washington DC: National Geographic, 2008.

Snedden, Robert. *Cell Division and Genetics*. Chicago, IL: Heinemann Library, 2008.

Van Gorp, Lynn. *Genetics*. Mankato, MN: Smart Apple, 2010.

Vaughan, Jenny. *Genetics*. Mankato, MN: Smart Apple, 2010.

WEB SITES

Due to the changing nature of Internet links, Rosen Publishing has developed an online list of Web sites related to the subject of this book. This site is updated regularly. Please use this link to access this list:

http://www.rosenlinks.com/scipa/gene

INDEX